W9-AHC-149

# SURVIVOR

# Crisis in Space
## Apollo 13

## Mark Beyer

Children's Press®
A Division of Scholastic Inc.
New York / Toronto / London / Auckland / Sydney
Mexico City / New Delhi / Hong Kong
Danbury, Connecticut

Book Design: Laura Stein and Christopher Logan
Diagrams: pp. 13, 16, 19, 33 by Christopher Logan
Contributing Editor: Matthew Pitt

Photo Credits: Cover (top and bottom), pp. 14, 21, 34 © Photri-Microstock; pp. 4, 8, 11, 24, 42 © Bettmann/Corbis; pp. 5, 9, 15, 25, 31, 33, 38, 39 © Photodisc; pp. 7, 36 © Corbis; pp. 29, 41 © TimePix; p. 30 © Bill Eppridge/TimePix

Library of Congress Cataloging-in-Publication Data

Beyer, Mark.
    Crisis in space : Apollo 13 / Mark Beyer.
        p. cm. — (Survivor)
    Includes bibliographical references and index.
    Summary: Recounts the events related to the ill-fated Apollo 13 mission and how the crew and mission control handled the in-flight crisis.
    ISBN 0-516-23903-1 (lib. bdg.) — ISBN 0-516-23485-4 (pbk.)
    1. Apollo 13 (Spacecraft)—Juvenile literature. 2. Project Apollo (U.S.)—Juvenile literature. 3. Space vehicle accidents—Juvenile literature. [1. Apollo 13 (Spacecraft) 2. Project Apollo (U.S.) 3. Space vehicle accidents] I. Title. II. Series.

    TL789.8.U6 A5215 2002
    629.45′4—dc21

                                                      2001042099

# Contents

# Introduction

Apollo 13 blasted off from the Kennedy Space Center in Cape Canaveral, Florida, on April 11, 1970. Commander Jim Lovell and pilots Jack Swigert and Fred Haise could hardly keep from grinning. In four days, they would become the third team of American astronauts to land on the moon. Jim Lovell held up a video camera and waved hello. He was sending a live image to Earth from 200,000 miles (321,860 km) away.

The TV networks didn't broadcast Lovell's space video. They figured that American audiences thought moon trips were old news. When Apollo 11 became the first manned spacecraft on the moon on July 20, 1969, it was an event that thrilled the whole world. Apollo 12 had also captured the public's imagination. Apollo 13

When Apollo 13 launched into space, its crew was in great spirits.

wasn't going to get as much press, but crew members didn't mind. They knew they weren't making history. They just wanted a smooth trip and wonderful memories.

What the crew got instead was a rough ride and a terrifying nightmare. On their third day in space, an oxygen tank exploded inside the *Odyssey* space capsule. From there, things only got worse. Suddenly, Americans were glued to their TV sets—but not to see a moon landing. They wanted to find out whether their space heroes would make it home safely. For the next four days, these astronauts lived out their nightmare. This is the story of their desperate race to return to Earth alive.

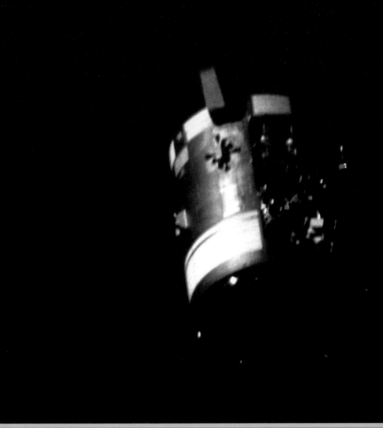

Americans followed the news about Apollo 13 for four days. They wanted to know if the troubled spacecraft would be able to return to Earth.

HOUR        MIN        SEC

# One

# Mission to the Moon

The National Aeronautic and Space Administration (NASA) had great plans for Apollo 13. It would be the most difficult of the three moon-landing missions. For one thing, the landing area would not be flat and smooth like those of Apollo 11 and Apollo 12. Scientists instead needed astronauts to land near hills. By collecting rocks and core samples, they would enable, or help, scientists to learn about the moon. The samples would reveal the moon's age and what it was made of.

## Unlucky 13?

Some people thought using the number 13 was unlucky. Strange sets of numbers connected with Apollo 13 gave superstitious people something to talk about. The mission was to begin at

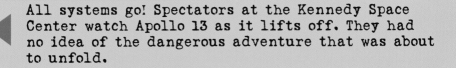

All systems go! Spectators at the Kennedy Space Center watch Apollo 13 as it lifts off. They had no idea of the dangerous adventure that was about to unfold.

1:13 P.M. on April 11. In military time (a twenty-four-hour clock), that number is written 13:13. Also, on April 13, the astronauts would enter the moon's orbit.

The people at NASA laughed at these superstitions. Apollo 13 did seem to have had bad luck, though. The original crew of Apollo 13 had been Alan Shepard, Stuart Roosa, and Edgar Mitchell. Their training, however, had fallen behind schedule. NASA didn't want to delay, or put off, Apollo 13, so they asked the Apollo 14 team of Commander Jim Lovell, Ken Mattingly, and Fred Haise to switch missions. The team jumped at the chance.

The bad luck continued. One week before the launch, backup pilot Charlie Duke caught German measles from his son. Duke had been in contact with all of the astronauts training for the mission. Lovell and Haise had already had the measles, so they were now immune. Being immune meant that they could not get the

 The astronauts of Apollo 13 (from left to right):
Jack Swigert, Jim Lovell, and Fred Haise.

disease again. Mattingly, however, had never had the measles. He could get sick during the mission.

NASA was forced to pull Mattingly from the mission. Rookie pilot Jack Swigert replaced Mattingly. Swigert trained hard for several days to catch up. With 48 hours left, Swigert was given the "okay" to fly. The new line-up was Lovell, Swigert, and Haise.

The flight plan was simple. A Saturn V rocket would blast the three astronauts into space. Jack Swigert would fly the Command Service Module (CSM) *Odyssey* from Earth's orbit to the moon's orbit. He would wait in moon orbit while Fred Haise piloted the Lunar Excursion Module (LEM) *Aquarius* down to the moon with Commander Jim Lovell. They would land at the feet of the Fra Mauro Hills for a 34-hour stay. Lovell and Haise would collect samples of moon rocks for the scientists to study. They would return to *Odyssey* with 200 pounds (90 kg) of samples. The three men would fly home aboard *Odyssey* and land in the ocean, mission accomplished.

That was the plan, anyway.

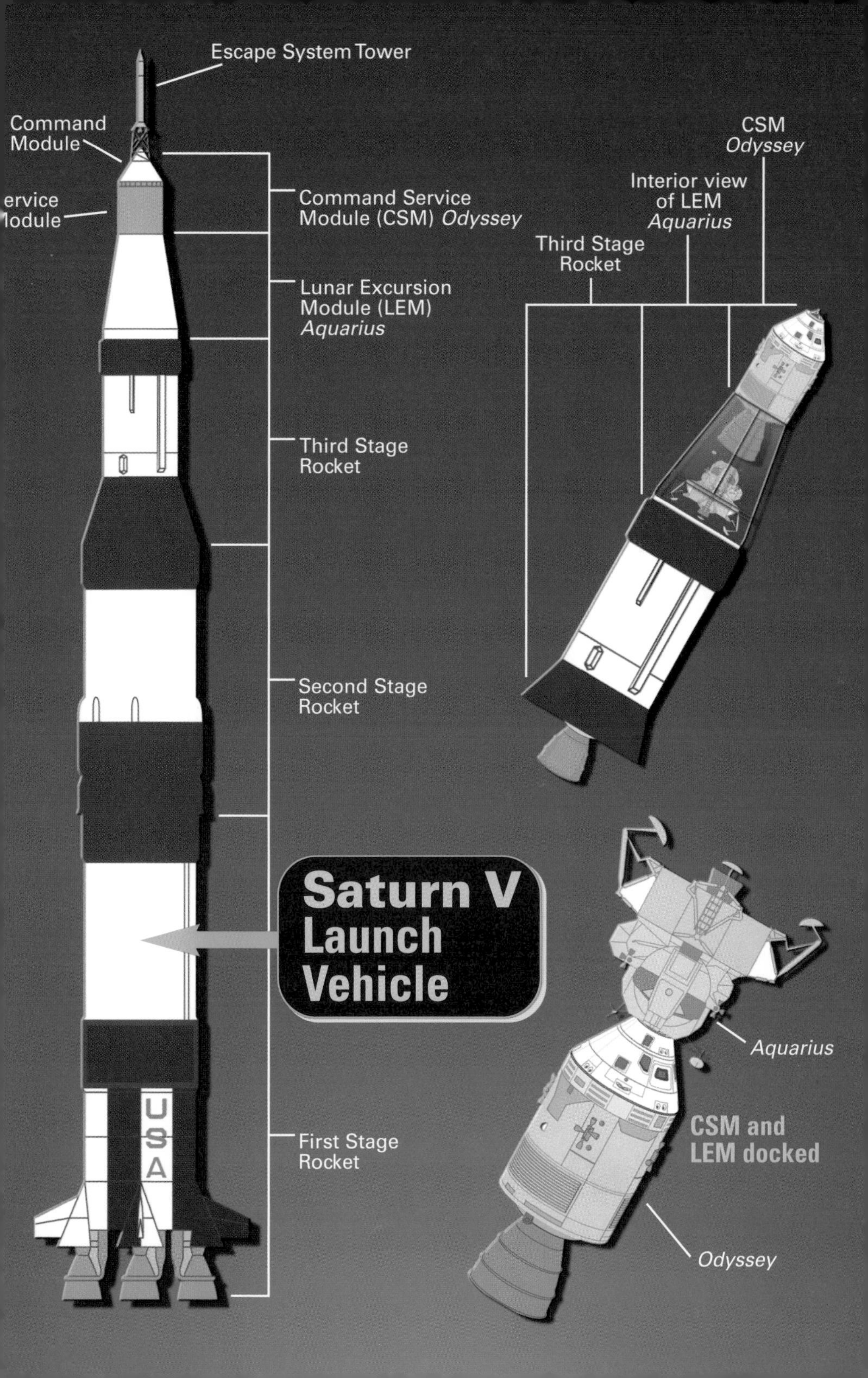

Escape System Tower

Command Module

Service Module

Command Service Module (CSM) *Odyssey*

Lunar Excursion Module (LEM) *Aquarius*

Third Stage Rocket

Second Stage Rocket

**Saturn V Launch Vehicle**

First Stage Rocket

USA

CSM *Odyssey*

Interior view of LEM *Aquarius*

Third Stage Rocket

*Aquarius*

**CSM and LEM docked**

*Odyssey*

# Two

# Brink of Disaster

On the morning of April 11, the three astronauts took an elevator up to the space capsule located atop the Saturn V rocket. They sat on the pilot's couch for the launch. Commander Jim Lovell sat on the left, Jack Swigert sat in the middle, and Fred Haise sat on the right. The command module had just enough room for the men and a few essential items. The crew's shoulders pressed together.

## Blast Off!

Mission control for all Apollo flights was stationed in Houston, Texas. Apollo 13 launched on schedule from Cape Canaveral, Florida. During radio transmissions, mission control was called "Houston" and Apollo 13 was called "13."

The lift-off of "13" from Cape Canaveral, Florida, went so smoothly that no one could have guessed the troubles ahead.

Through radar monitors, Houston would be able to follow 13's every move—even when 13 reached the moon, 200,000 miles (321,860 km) away. Houston watched the monitors as the giant Saturn V rocket lifted into the blue sky.

Just outside Earth's atmosphere, the rocket's first stage fell away. The second stage had five engines that fired the rocket farther into space. The center engine, however, cut out too quickly.

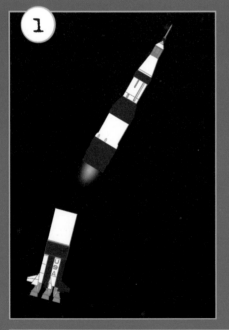

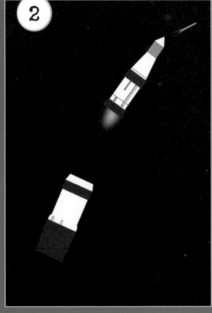

1. Saturn V's first stage falls away. Then, the center engine of the second stage misfires.

2. The escape system tower breaks away as planned. Saturn V's second stage successfully falls away. Everything is A-OK!

This was 13's first glitch. Commander Lovell asked Houston a tough question: Should he abort, or stop, the flight?

Houston quickly gave the go-ahead to stay with the rocket. They decided to burn the four remaining engines longer than normal. This method would keep the ship on course and safe. When the second stage fell away, the third-stage rocket would burn longer, too. Apollo 13 was now shooting out of Earth's orbit at 2,000 miles (3,218 km) per hour.

Lovell shut down the third-stage engine. Other than the second-stage problem, the lift-off had gone perfectly. The ship was pointed in the right direction. It was time to separate the CSM *Odyssey* from the rocket booster and connect it to the LEM *Aquarius*.

## Docking Odyssey with Aquarius

Four hours after lift-off, Jack Swigert took the pilot's couch, switching places with Commander Lovell. Swigert disconnected *Odyssey* from the rocket booster. He used small thrusters outside the ship to turn *Odyssey* around. Inside the booster sat the LEM *Aquarius*. Swigert fired the thrusters and slowly moved into docking position. The nose of *Odyssey* had a metal probe that fit into a portal, or opening, atop *Aquarius*. Slowly and smoothly, Swigert piloted *Odyssey* into *Aquarius*. Once connected, he reversed the thrusters and pulled *Aquarius* from the booster. He then turned the connected ships around to face the path they would take to the moon.

Thirty-one hours into the flight, the crew burned *Odyssey*'s main engine to change course. This engine burn put the ship on target to enter the moon's orbit. Afterward, the crew sat back in the cozy capsule. They watched the ship's progress, ate, and rested. All was well aboard Apollo 13. However, on the third day, everything would change.

**1** The CSM *Odyssey* separates from the third stage. Meanwhile, large panels break off into space, exposing the LEM *Aquarius*.

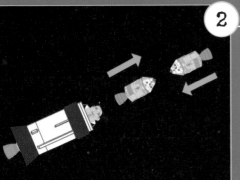

**2** *Odyssey* moves away from third stage and turns nose-first back toward *Aquarius*. Following a straight path, *Odyssey* docks with *Aquarius*.

**3** Now connected with *Aquarius*, *Odyssey* backs away and pulls *Aquarius* out of the third stage. The third stage floats away into space.

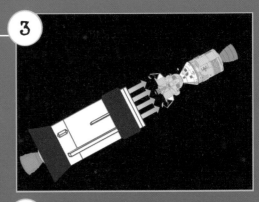

**4** Using its thrusters, *Odyssey* turns the joined unit around. With *Aquarius* in front, *Odyssey* powers the unit toward the moon.

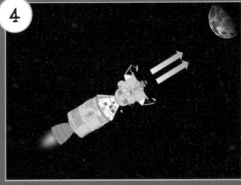

CRISIS IN SPACE: APOLLO 13

# Explosion!

Now that they were on course, the crew had time for some fun. They floated through the tunnel between *Odyssey* and *Aquarius*. They did somersaults inside the small, zero-gravity capsule. They drank huge droplets of floating water. After the fun, they got back to business. Lovell and Haise stayed on *Aquarius* to close the tunnel. Swigert went into *Odyssey* and contacted Houston.

Houston wanted the crew to do some routine systems checks before going to bed. One job was to stir the super-cold liquid oxygen in two huge tanks. These tanks of liquid oxygen were crucial to 13's success. They supplied the crew with air and the ship with battery power. The tanks sat inside the belly of *Odyssey's* service module. Swigert got the request from Houston for the stir. He flipped the two switches on the control panel and waited. Houston waited for their computers to detect the stir.

Suddenly, a loud booming noise sounded through *Odyssey*. Something had exploded inside the service module. The ship began to wobble. Warning lights on the control panel lit up and a buzzer sounded. Houston quickly asked, "What happened, 13?"

Haise and Lovell raced in from *Aquarius*. Lovell sounded worried as he asked, "What happened?"

After an explosion damaged Apollo 13's oxygen tanks, the crew found themselves in a race against the clock.

"I don't know," Swigert replied. "I just stirred the tanks."

There was no time to find out what caused the explosion. The crew needed to gain control of their ship and check the damage. Lovell sat in the pilot's seat. He used *Odyssey*'s thrusters to try to steady the ship's movements. But each time he corrected the wobble, the ship turned the other way.

Meanwhile, Swigert and Haise checked the control panel. What they saw chilled them. Oxygen tank one was empty, and the levels in tank two were dropping fast. Their life-supporting supply of oxygen was quickly leaking away. The control panel showed more bad news. Their battery power was also draining. Part of the oxygen was used with hydrogen to create the ship's power. Without the necessary oxygen, the batteries could not be charged. The ship's lights, heater, and computers were quickly using up battery power!

The crew was in grave danger and knew it. If they turned toward Earth now, it would take days to make it back. Yet *Odyssey* had only a few hours of oxygen and power left. Once out of oxygen, the men would suffocate. They had to stop the leaking oxygen and power loss immediately. It was their only chance of getting home alive.

Lovell realized that, thousands of miles away, mission control was waiting for a report. He cleared his throat and called down to Earth. "Houston, we've had a problem."

# Three

# Help from Mission Control

In Houston, mission control flight commander Gene Kranz asked his technicians what had happened and how it could be fixed.

"We don't know yet," they answered. All they did know was that the mission to the moon was over. Landing on the moon was the furthest thing from the minds of the technicians. Saving the lives of three brave men was all that mattered now.

## Saving Odyssey

Houston told 13 to shut down the valves that let oxygen mix with hydrogen. This mixture charged the batteries. If shutting down valves stopped the leak, the crew could survive for a few days. The crew shut down the valves, then watched

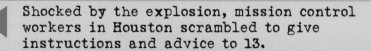

Shocked by the explosion, mission control workers in Houston scrambled to give instructions and advice to 13.

the levels on the control panel—no luck. The oxygen continued leaking.

Houston technicians searched desperately for another answer. Suddenly, they thought of the Lunar Excursion Module. *Aquarius* was still attached to *Odyssey*. It had its own batteries and oxygen supply. The supply would keep two people alive for two days. To make it safely back to Earth, *Aquarius* would now have to support three men for four days. There were no other options. If the astronauts were to survive, this plan had to work.

Houston laid out the plan to the crew. The crew nodded, then rushed to power up *Aquarius*. Lovell, Haise, and Swigert had 15 minutes to get *Aquarius* up and running before *Odyssey* shut down and died. They knew their spacecraft would become their coffin if they didn't make every second count.

# Did you know?

Gravity is the force that holds you down on Earth. In space, there is zero gravity. When a rocket speeds up to 5,000 miles (8,000 km) per hour, it can shut its engines off without decreasing its speed. There is no gravity to slow it down. Therefore, a rocket only needs to burn its engines until it reaches the speed it wants to fly. As long as the rocket is headed in the right direction, no more engine power is needed to continue flying.

## Shutdown and "Lifeboat"

*Aquarius* was a great lifeboat, but it could not be used to reenter Earth's atmosphere. The crew needed *Odyssey*'s heat shield for that. The key to saving *Odyssey* was shutting it down for now. This would save what little battery power and oxygen *Odyssey* had left. They would need *Odyssey*'s last scraps of power when they tried to reenter Earth's atmosphere.

Lovell, Haise, and Swigert began transferring computer data from *Odyssey* to *Aquarius*. *Aquarius* needed this data to fly correctly. Without it, the crew wouldn't know where to steer. The crew completed the transfer with minutes to spare. Swigert stayed in *Odyssey* long enough to shut down all systems. He then floated through the tunnel and into the cramped *Aquarius*.

*Odyssey* was stable, for now. Shutting down all of its power had worked. It was no longer leaking oxygen or draining battery power. *Aquarius* was the astronauts' lifeboat. If they used little power and oxygen, they estimated that they had four days to live. They began to figure out how to get home.

Cramped conditions, chilling temperatures, darkness, and a low oxygen supply on 13 made time seem to crawl.

# Four

# Homeward Bound

Back on Earth, people tuned in and watched the TV news in stunned silence. The reports were streaming in—Apollo 13 was in deep trouble. Americans wanted information and answers. Would the crew run out of air? Would they make it home alive?

These were questions mission control was asking, too. Houston had two options to get 13 home. The first was to have the ship head home right away. The second was to send the ship around the moon to help it gain speed. That speed would carry *Aquarius* to Earth on a free return, without using up its rocket fuel.

Houston decided that heading home now was too risky. *Aquarius*'s engine was too small and didn't have enough fuel. Houston didn't know if

During the crisis, Marilyn Lovell could only sit and wait—hoping her husband would soon return to her.

*Odyssey*'s engine would work at all. If the engine had been damaged by the blast, it could explode! Then the crew would perish for sure. Sending the ship around the moon was the best option for getting Lovell, Haise, and Swigert back to Earth safely.

A trip around the moon meant the crew couldn't get to Earth for four days. They had just enough oxygen and food for the journey. Battery power was still a problem. The crew needed to shut down most of the power in *Aquarius*. They gathered all the water they could, and waited for instructions.

## Slingshot Around the Moon

Apollo 13 needed to fire *Aquarius*'s engine to get on course for a free return. At 2:44 A.M. on April 14, the crew fired the engine for 30 seconds. This increased their speed. More important, it changed their direction slightly. The moon's gravity would now throw 13 around the dark side and fling it back toward Earth. As they circled the moon, the crew gazed down at its surface. They were 158 miles (254 km) above the moon—the closest they would come. Now, they were counting on the moon to help rescue them.

As the ship rounded the moon, Houston discovered another problem. Even with the power shut down, there was still not enough battery power to last four days in space. Water to cool

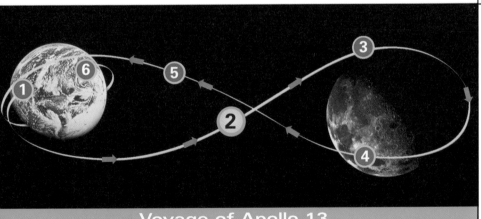

**Voyage of Apollo 13**

1. Launch
2. Oxygen tank explodes
3. Engines fired to enter moon's gravity
4. Engines fired again—need speed to get home
5. Deadly $CO_2$ levels
6. Reentry

the equipment would also run out by then. *Aquarius* needed to increase its speed to get home 10 hours earlier than planned.

*Aquarius*'s big engine was supposed to be used for landing on the moon. Now the crew needed it to boost the ship toward home. Lovell and Haise fired the engine for more than 4 minutes after *Aquarius* passed behind the moon. This burn increased their speed by 586 miles (943 km) per hour. Apollo 13 would splash down in the Pacific

 An exhausted Fred Haise takes a much-needed water break.

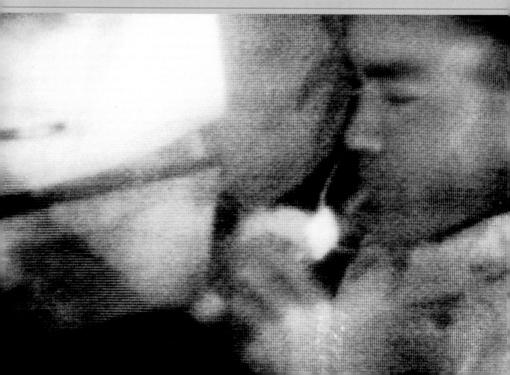

Ocean two days and 15 hours later—if the plan worked. The crew looked at each other nervously, knowing what would happen if it didn't.

## Cold Days in Space

The crew was exhausted. Eighteen hours had passed since they had last slept. More work was yet to come, though. More problems would need to be solved. They needed to rest, so they tried sleeping in shifts. Lovell stayed awake first, while Haise and Swigert went into the darkened *Odyssey* to sleep. It was bitterly cold on *Odyssey*, just above freezing. Water built up on the windows and walls. The crew could see their breath. No one slept for more than 2 hours at a time.

## Poison Control

Houston noticed another problem as the ship sailed closer to Earth. The carbon dioxide levels inside *Aquarius* were building. Carbon dioxide in large doses can be poisonous to humans.

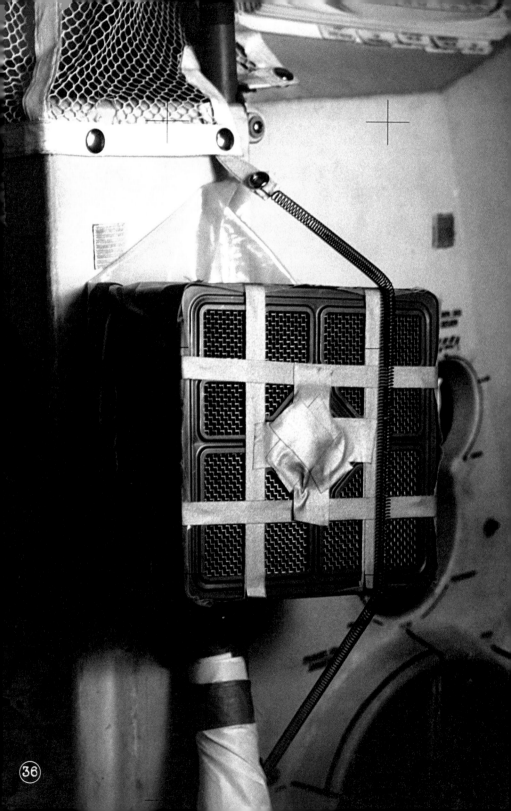

As humans inhale oxygen, they exhale carbon dioxide. *Aquarius* had filters to recycle the carbon dioxide. *Aquarius* was designed for only two men, though. Having three men inside the lifeboat was more than the filters could handle. If the carbon dioxide levels rose too high, the crew would be poisoned and die.

The crew needed to replace the filters with filters from *Odyssey*. The problem was that *Odyssey*'s filters were square and *Aquarius*'s filters were round! In under an hour, Houston came up with a way for the crew to rig the square filters to fit in the round ones. The astronauts used a plastic bag, tape, cardboard, and a hose to change the filter. The rigging worked! Each crew member took a welcome, well-earned gulp of air.

Using a few household items, Houston and the crew were able to construct a device that kept the astronauts alive.

# Five

## Splashdown!

It was two days after the explosion on *Odyssey*. In one more day, it would be time to reenter Earth's atmosphere—the hardest test of all. The crew huddled together to stay warm. They ate to keep up their strength.

In Houston, technicians worked in flight simulators. These are machines that recreate the conditions in space (like zero gravity). Mission control had to figure out a way for the crew to turn the power on in *Odyssey* without draining the batteries. Time and again they failed to find the bare minimum of power that was needed.

With only hours to spare, they found the solution. Houston told the crew to connect an emergency power line from *Aquarius* to *Odyssey*. This line let them transfer *Aquarius*'s remaining

Though Earth was a welcome sight, the astronauts of 13 still had no idea if they would survive reentry.

battery power to *Odyssey*. Now they had enough power to turn on the computer and other electronic systems inside *Odyssey*.

## Module Separation and Reentry

Houston was worried about *Odyssey*'s heat shield. If the explosion had cracked the shield, the ship would burn up in the atmosphere. There was no way to know if the shield was damaged before reentry. They had no choice but to take that risk.

Swigert sat on the pilot's couch and separated *Odyssey's* command module from its service module, where the oxygen tank had exploded. As the module floated away, the crew saw the

**Did you know?**

*A spacecraft's heat shield reaches 5,000 degrees Fahrenheit (2,760 degrees Celsius) during reentry into Earth's atmosphere.*

damage of the explosion. A panel covering a third of the module was missing. The area inside the panel was black and burned.

Next, Swigert separated *Odyssey* from *Aquarius*. The crew's lifeboat drifted away. As it tumbled through the vacuum of space, a crew member remarked, "Good-bye, *Aquarius*, and we thank you." *Odyssey* picked up speed as it entered Earth's atmosphere. While they welcomed the sight of Earth, they knew their nightmare wasn't over yet. There were just 8 hours of power left on the ship, and it was time to test the heat shield.

# Splashdown!

During reentry, there are 4 minutes when communication is lost between Houston and a spacecraft. Those 4 minutes stretched to nearly 5 during Apollo 13's reentry. *Odyssey* dropped through the atmosphere at more than 7 miles (11 km) per second. In the South Pacific, an aircraft carrier waited to pick up the astronauts.

The Apollo 13 astronauts returned to Earth and received a hero's welcome. Here, the crew stands with President Richard Nixon.

After nearly 5 minutes of unbearable silence, pilot Jack Swigert said, "Okay!" over the radio. America breathed a sigh of relief. Three parachutes opened above the *Odyssey* and the craft gently floated into the ocean. The astronauts were home. They had survived great danger and beaten impossible odds.

## After the Mission

NASA investigated the oxygen tank explosion during the months following Apollo 13's return. Tests proved that a faulty coil inside one of the tanks caused the spark that ignited the tanks. *Odyssey*'s oxygen tanks had been used on several other space missions.

In the face of tragedy, the astronauts and Houston's mission control stayed calm. They worked nonstop in the days following the explosion. Mission control worked to keep the Apollo 13 crew alive. The astronauts did all they could to fly the spacecraft and remain hopeful. Together, mission control and the crew prevented what could have been a tragic disaster.

**abort**  to stop a flight

**Apollo**  the name given to a series of space missions to the moon

**astronaut**  a person who travels beyond Earth's atmosphere

**carbon dioxide**  the gas that is produced when humans breathe out

**Command Service Module (CSM)**  a space vehicle used to fly into space and orbit the Earth or moon

**enable**  to help someone get something done

**gravity**  the force that holds down objects on Earth

**immune**  being able to resist a disease

**Lunar Excursion Module (LEM)**  a space vehicle used only to land on the moon

**National Aeronautic and Space Administration (NASA)**  the government organization that conducts space research and missions

**orbit**  to circle around a planet or moon

**simulators**  machines that recreate the conditions in space

Baker, David. *Danger on Apollo 13*. Vero Beach, Florida: Rourke Enterprises, 1988.

Cole, Michael D. *Apollo 13: Space Emergency*. New York: Enslow Publishers, 1995.

Hasday, Judy L. and James Scott Brady. *The Apollo 13 Mission*. New York: Chelsea House Publishers, 2000.

# RESOURCES

## ORGANIZATIONS
*www.nasa.gov*
National Aeronautics and Space Administration
(NASA) 300 E Street, S.W. Washington, DC 20546
Get news about upcoming flights and missions, and
learn about jobs at NASA.

## WEB SITES
### SPACE.com
*www.space.com*
Photo galleries, cool facts, amazing games—this Web
site has everything!

### Kennedy Space Center: Apollo 13
*www.ksc.nasa.gov/history/apollo/apollo-13/
apollo-13.html*
This site gives you all the facts of the Apollo 13 mission. Learn more about what the astronauts did to
survive in space.

### Space Camp
*www.spacecamp.com*
Learn about a space camp where you can work inside
flight simulators and even experience zero gravity.

# INDEX

## ABOUT THE AUTHOR

Mark Beyer is a freelance writer living in Florida. He has had a fascination with space flight since the age of six in 1969, when he watched Apollo 11 fly to the moon and set an astronaut on the moon's surface.